The Most Unusual Pet Ever,

Henry our Great Blue Heron

and his adventures

The Most Unusual Pet Ever,
Henry our Great Blue Heron
and his adventures

WRITTEN BY **Sondra Perry**

ILLUSTRATED BY **Janice Byer**

JABBERWOCKY MINNEAPOLIS

Jabberwocky Press
212 3rd Avenue North, Suite 290
Minneapolis, MN 55401
612.455.2293
www.Jabberwocky-Books.com

Juvenile non fiction/animals/pets

ISBN - 978-1-935204-22-0
LCCN - 2010942895

Cover Design & Typeset by Kristeen Wegner
Illustrations by Janice Byer

A portion of every book sold will go toward the building of the Shepherd's Gate Life Center in Livermore, California.

W W W . **HENRY** T H E **GREAT** B L U E **HERON** . C O M

Printed in the United States of America
CPSIA facility code: BP 306125

Jabberwocky
Books

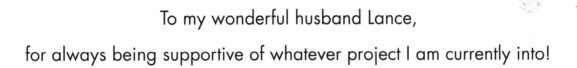

To my wonderful husband Lance,

for always being supportive of whatever project I am currently into!

And to George and Sammy for putting up with the sight and smell

of thawing fish in the sink for the past seven years!

I want to make a special mention of the women and children of

Shepherd's Gate who have reminded me how precious a simple smile or hug

really is and that everyone just wants someone to be glad to see them!

They have also reminded me first-hand just how much kids love to be read to.

Even if they only let you get to page number two before

running to get another book!

The Most Unusual Pet Ever,

Henry our Great Blue Heron

and his adventures

Well, hi there!
Thank you for wanting to know more about our "unusual pet," Henry ...

You cannot put him on a leash or take him for a walk.

He does not come when you call his name
and you cannot put him in a cage.

You cannot give him a bath or pet him.

He does not sit next to you on the couch
or sleep besides you at night.

He will never come into the house and
could never be taken to the veterinarian!

He does not wear a collar with his name and "if found"
information around his neck.

You also do not have to follow him and pick up his poop either!

THEN HOW IN THE WORLD
CAN YOU CALL HIM A PET?!

Well we can, and do,
and once you read this you will see how,
and realize that a special friend or pet
can come in many forms,
so it's best to stay alert so you don't miss them!

So sit back, relax, and enjoy the story!

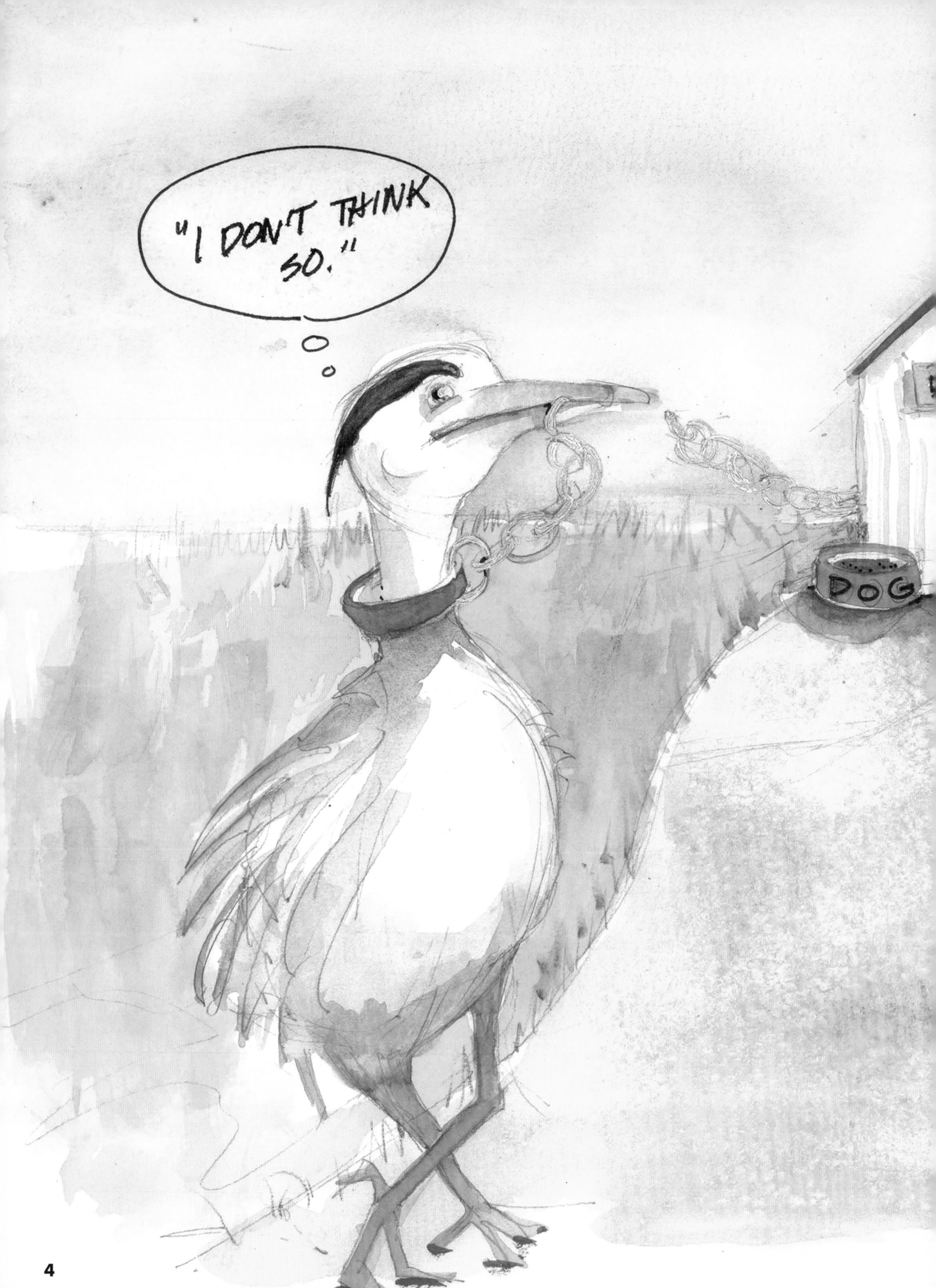
"I DON'T THINK SO."
DOG

The day
we first met
Henry

It was a normal morning at the Perry house.

My husband Lance and my two step kids, George (age 12) and Samantha (age 8) were still in bed. We live in a quiet neighborhood in San Ramon, California, about twenty-five miles east of San Francisco. Our house sits on a corner with a big backyard and two ponds FILLED WITH FISH (this will become a very important part of the story). Like I mentioned, it was a normal morning ... I was making coffee when all of a sudden, from the corner of my eye, I notice something BIG and MOVING! I look outside and almost SCREAM! Outside, by the smaller pond is a HUGH BIRD—I think! It looks six feet tall! What is it?

I run to get my camera. (No one is going to believe this, I'm thinking. I need PROOF!) I race to the back door with my camera, JUST AS THE "THING" is flying away! The wings on this thing stretch six feet across and its long legs are dangling behind as it flies away. Oh, what a site! What was that? It was SO BIG! I reach for the "Bird Identification" book to find out. Usually I am looking up the name of some cute little birdie with red on his head or yellow on his belly.

But flipping it open now I'm thinking something BIG and PREHISTORIC! You know how our imaginations can go wild sometimes … And then I see it, IT was a GREAT BLUE HERON! Wow! How cool is that?—right in our own backyard. Will IT EVER COME BACK?! I wondered.

Turns out I had nothing to worry about. And like they say, "Don't waste time worrying about something before there is even something to worry about!"

The bird is back!
The Five-Day Battle

To my surprise and delight, the Bird was back at the pond within about five minutes! Turns out this Bird was about FOUR feet tall, not SIX … but hey, that's still BIG! For a BIRD! In your YARD! Now the rest of the family is up and can see it for themselves; I didn't need the proof of a photograph after all.

We are all excited to see this BIG BIRD in our yard, until … we realize, IT'S AFTER THE FISH IN THE POND! IT just grabbed one; it's in ITS MOUTH. Ohhh nooooooo!

THAT BIRD JUST SWALLOWED ONE OF OUR FISH! We run out and shoo the Bird away! The Bird flies away... the Bird comes back... We repeated this process over and over again for DAYS! We even laid screens across the ponds to keep IT out, but we were afraid the Bird would get its legs caught in between the screens, and NO ONE wants to see a large bird stuck!

Where did all the *fish* go?

After several days of this, the Bird had pretty much eaten all of the fish from BOTH PONDS! The remaining fish were so afraid they stayed hidden and would not even come to the surface to eat THEIR food! I BET THEY FELT LIKE THEY WERE THE FOOD AND IT WAS PROBABLY JUST A TRICK TO GET THEM TO COME OUT SO THE BIRD COULD EAT THEM! I don't blame them.

Now even though this Bird was eating our fish, he wasn't being mean to us, that's just what GREAT BLUE HERONS do—they eat fish! And here we have two big "food bowls" just waiting! What a good find for the Bird; and for us too, it turns out.

The
first fish

"Wow, this Bird sure gets an 'A' for effort and persistence," I said. My husband says, "This Bird must really be hungry." And then before he knows what he is about to get us—ME— into, he says, "Maybe we should go buy the Bird a fish at the grocery store, that might keep IT away from the fish in the ponds." And that is how it began. We went to the store. We bought a four-pack of trout (head on and everything). We laid one out on the grass. We watched as the Bird quickly grabbed it up with its long beak and swallowed the trout whole!

So now we are IN IT! The Bird had flown away after eating the trout, leaving the ponds alone. Had it worked? Maybe? It seemed to be because the Bird kept coming back. But only in the morning for a snack of one fish and then would fly away, leaving the ponds alone. After four days of this I was out of fish. I guess I need to get more, to be ready IF the Bird comes back tomorrow, right? And so I went back to the store and bought another four-pack of trout. I was never quite sure how long this would last. Well, that was seven years ago!

22

"The *bird*" should have a *name*

We did not know if the Bird was a girl or a boy, but we "felt" like IT was a boy, so we named the Bird "Henry," the Great Blue Heron. Apparently the males are about 10 percent bigger than the females but we have no other Heron to compare Henry to so, HE'S A BOY … to us anyway.

Getting to
know
each other

Well, Henry and I both startled each other a lot in the beginning. I would get startled as I opened the curtains in the morning to find this BIG BIRD sitting right outside the window on top of the barbecue or table. Henry would get surprised by the sudden opening of the curtains. Frightened and all crazy-like, he would open his wings and half-fly, half-fall off the barbecue or table. Who knows how long he had been waiting there. He's probably been sleeping! Henry would then regain his composure and come back to staring through the window, looking at me, just waiting. Where's my fish? he seemed to be saying. All this before I've had my coffee! Too early in the morning for such things! But I am always happy to see him there waiting for me to feed him.

Our *feeding routine* begins

But in a short time we got used to each other's presence and settled into our "routine." I would open the curtains slowly. Henry would get into position, walking towards the corner of the grass. I give a little tap on the glass door and open it. I talk to Henry as I come out to greet him, saying his name and asking how he is. Then I drop the fish on the corner of the grass and as I turn to go back into the house, Henry grabs it up with his long beak. He then stretches his neck out and down it goes, HEAD FIRST. Sometimes Henry flies or runs to the pond with the fish in his mouth and "dips it" into the pond first before swallowing it! It's quite entertaining! Especially watching this big Bird with long legs running with a fish hanging out its mouth!

Fish, *fish,* and **more** *fish!*

In the last seven years we have gone through A LOT of fish. You see, you cannot get trout at the pet food store! So now the clerks at our grocery store are used to the twenty pound trout order and know the crazy story. I am often asked, while standing in line with a large box of trout, "How are you going to prepare that?" And again, I share the story with a stranger who probably thinks I am crazy! The things we do for the ones we love! But I will tell you a fact: it's always worth it!

Sometimes Henry...

Just like any other "pet," Henry has his quirks and a personality all his own.

Sometimes Henry:

- Stands on the fence.
- Stands on the basketball hoop.
- Stands on the vegetables in my Husband's garden. This was always followed by getting shooed off the vegetables!
- Stands on the roof or chimney for the day.
- Eats quickly and then just flies away.
- Hangs out all day, staring at us through the back door.
- Acts shy.
- Acts like he wants more fish.
- Twists his body and shakes his feathers—he looks four times his size when he does that.

- Sharpens his beak on the edge of the pond.
- Grooms himself with his beak.
- Stands at attention, tilting his head, looking up into the sky. Maybe he sees someone he knows?
- Patiently looks into the pond all day, hoping for a fish perhaps?
- Suns himself for hours.
- Stands on one foot, sleeping I think, then stretches his wings out, one at a time, just to wake himself up.
- Curls his long neck into an S shape and rests his head on his body.
- Makes a "FRAWK" sound. Is he scared, talking, or wanting more fish??

And then SOMETIMES Henry will not show up for a few days!

Henry, *famous?*

On the days when Henry wouldn't show up for his fish, we would wonder, Where IS he? Free fish, silly bird! How can he pass that up? He must be doing something very important. Maybe visiting friends or family? On a vacation? And then we started to realize all the times we had seen Henry's likeness and in so many different places.

ON CALENDARS!
GREETING CARDS!
POSTCARDS!
ON SOCKS AND T-SHIRTS!
SCULPTURES!
PAINTINGS!
GARDEN DECOYS!
BINOCULAR ADVERTISEMENTS!
OCEANSIDE HOTEL LOGOS!
ROAD SIGNS!
JEWELRY!
BIRD BINGO!
THERE IS EVEN A GREAT BLUE HERON BEER!

Henry is everywhere! And that's when we realized where he must be when he doesn't show up to get his morning fish. HENRY'S AT A PHOTO SHOOT GETTING HIS PICTURE TAKEN OR PAINTED. He must be a model: Henry is FAMOUS!

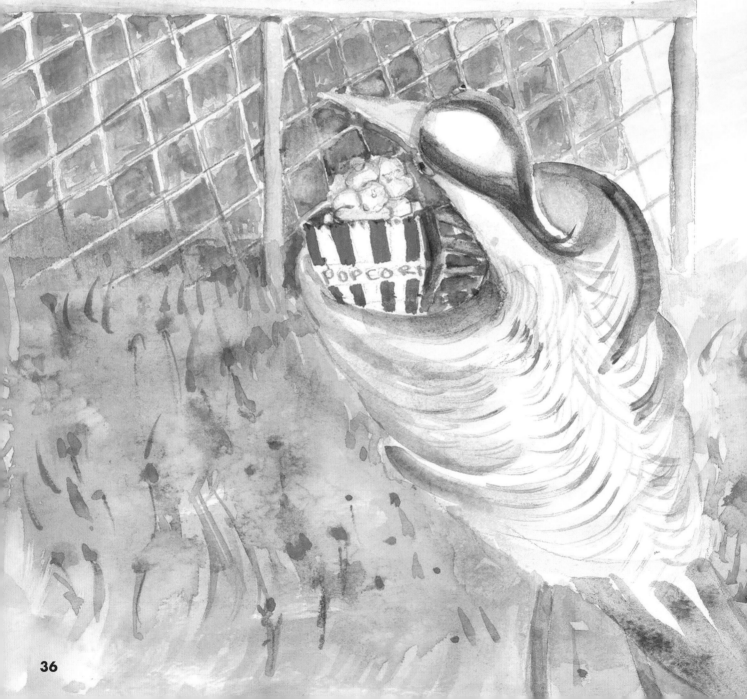

Does **Henry** think he is at the "**People Zoo?**"

On many days Henry will just hang out on the patio, starring at us through the sliding glass doors. It makes you wonder what is going through his mind. He's acting like he's at the Zoo or something.

Just think about it:

- He flies in.
- Stares at the humans on display, observing them through the glass door. Just waiting for a human to do something worth looking at. Oh look, that one is eating. Oh, that one is cleaning the kitchen—again!?
- Places his "snack" order by staring through the kitchen window.
- He swallows his snack while still looking at the humans on display.
- He then gets a beverage, a sip of water at the pond.
- After he tires of the scene, he flies away!

Sounds very much like a trip to the zoo to me!

Henry and the ducks

Just like any other pet, Henry now thinks this is HIS yard and does not take kindly to another animal or WATER BIRD getting fed through HIS backdoor! Two years ago, in the Spring, two mallard ducks decided to land in our backyard and started hanging out during the day, lounging about the ponds and eating cracked corn (fed to them through the back door). They would leave in the late afternoon and return in the morning. WELL, this did not sit well at all with Henry. Henry would glare at them, sticking his beak out and standing tall, cornering them to one side of the pond. I was always so surprised to see the two ducks back the next day, especially since they were not being treated very nicely by that Great Blue Heron. The two ducks stayed on for a few weeks and then flew away. We have seen these ducks for two Spring seasons in a row now, who knows if they will be back again next Spring? I hope so. Henry will just have to work on his manners! There is enough food for everyone, and hey, he doesn't even LIKE cracked corn. I've told him this many times!!

Henry and the chickens!

Yep! Chickens! To help with the garden we brought home three chickens. We call them Mother, Raven and Braveheart. They hang out in the garden eating bugs and fertilizing as they go. We think of the three girls as Henry's sisters. Now for some reason Henry is much nicer to "his sisters" than he was to the visiting ducks. By "nicer" I mean he basically ignores them! Thank goodness because they LIVE here and it's so much better when everyone can just get along. Henry must know that even though these birds have feathers they are not "water birds" and will not be in competition for his fish. Or maybe he has matured!

I wish
I could **talk** to him

Just like everyone does with their pets, "I think", whenever I am around Henry, I talk to him.

"How are you today, Henry?"; "Where have you been?"; "Did you sleep well in the rain last night?"; "Where do you go when you fly away from here?"; "How old are you?"; "Do you have other families to visit, do they feed you too?"; "Where do you live?"; "Do you sleep in a nest?"; "Do you have a family?"; "Are you a girl or a boy?"

Wouldn't it be great if you could talk to your pet or any animal for just five minutes? Just think of what you would ask! I wonder what THEY would ask you?! Better make it ten minutes!!

Just *glad* to know *you*

But for now, I am happy to "talk" to Henry using actions and behaviors. Unless someone comes up with some kind of "animal-human communication device," what other choice do I have, right? I feel he is happy when I see Henry flying in, eagerly looking for his fish. It says to me, *"I am happy, healthy, hungry, and glad to know where I can get a free meal"*! And when Henry stands by the pond on one leg, with his head comfortably in an S shape, resting on his body for so many hours that he has to "stretch" his wings out just to stand up straight, I see that he is comfortable and relaxed. And that makes me happy; even with no words exchanged, I can "hear it" through his actions. And I hope Henry can also "hear and feel" what I cannot speak to him. Through my smile and pleasant tone when I chatter at him, I hope he knows that I am always happy to see him, care about him, and feel blessed by his presence.

He's *still wild*

Now, we know and respect the fact that Henry is a "wild bird" and never want him to stop fending for himself. It would not be good for Henry to only rely on us for his food. So we give him a snack when he comes over and feel good to see Henry still hunting for food. In the yard he finds bugs, snails, and grubs. Sometimes I think he might be trying to cover up his "fish breath" with bugs. Bugs just might be *mints* in the bird world! Just think of what would happen if his "Heron friends" ever caught on to his secret fish spot. He's got to keep this to himself! Henry still looks in the pond for more fish. There have not been any fish in there since he ate them all. But it's fun to watch him; he will stare into it, patiently waiting to see one swimming by. I guess he has not given up hope—as none of us ever should!

Have you *ever* seen a *great* blue heron?

Even with all the streams, golf courses with ponds and the many miles of "open space" reserved for wildlife around us, I had never noticed such a bird right in our own neighborhood. And I'm sure there are more just like him. Henry has reminded me to always: Look up! Look down! Look all around! Look in the trees. Look in the bushes! Look up in the sky!

It is amazing what treasures of nature are all around us. All you have to do is STOP, LOOK, and LISTEN. And soon you will see and hear what has always been there, so quietly going about their business. Birds and bugs and butterflies too! You never know what you might see; you just have to look.

About the Author

Sondra Perry lives in San Ramon, CA, with her husband Lance, a great blue heron, three chickens and occasionaly two ducks. George is now 19 and in college and Sammantha is 16. Having once been a chef with a catering company and then a maker and distributer of handmade soaps, Sondra has now turned her talents toward being an author of children's books. She continues to volunteer in the daycare center of Shepherds Gate.   sondra.perry4@gmail.com

About the Illustrator

Janice Byer is an award-winning Fine Artist living in the San Francisco Bay Area, active in watercolor, oil, and pastel. She has received her Bachelor's of Fine Arts degree from the California College of Arts and Crafts in Oakland, CA, with drawing as her major. As a children's book illustrator, Janice's style is soft, sensitive and delightfully charming.   www.artistjanicebyer.com

To see more photos and videos of the Real Henry, check out:

WWW.**HENRY**THE**GREAT**BLUE**HERON**.COM

Henry, our Great Blue Heron